93rd U.S. Open
Baltusrol Golf Club

Writer
Larry Dorman

Photographers
Lawrence Levy
Michael C. Cohen

Editor
Bev Norwood

ISBN 1-878843-08-7

©1993 United States Golf Association®
Golf House, Far Hills, New Jersey 07931

Statistics produced by Unisys Corporation

Course illustration by Libby Peper

Published by International Merchandising Corporation,
One Erieview Plaza, Cleveland, Ohio 44114

Designed and produced by Davis Design

Printed in the United States of America

I was impressed by Lee Janzen long before he won the U.S. Open — and I might even claim a little credit for his victory. Perhaps Jack Nicklaus and I tuned him up a bit when we played a practice round prior to this year's Memorial Tournament with Lee and our mutual friend, Rocco Mediate. That was just two weeks before the Open.

In any event, I was not surprised, and I was very pleased, when Lee played so well at Baltusrol and that he held the lead in the closing rounds against some very strong opponents.

This is the ninth annual commemorative book on the U.S. Open, produced by our friends at Rolex Watch USA. The purpose of this book is to document the 1993 championship in words and color photographs. All proceeds are to be directed to the USGA Members Program for activities to benefit junior golf.

Arnold Palmer

Arnold Palmer

93rd U.S. Open
Baltusrol Golf Club

Throughout the 93-year history of the U.S. Open, golf clubs that have hosted the event have been named after Greek gods, a near-sighted baseball team, a mythical mountain and a sacred city in the Arab world. Students of the U.S. Golf Association's championship rota would be able to identify them as Winged Foot, Myopia Hunt Club, Olympic Club and Medinah.

The rich history of the origins of those clubs certainly bears noting. But for sheer uniqueness and originality of name, no club in America can match Baltusrol Golf Club, site of the 1993 Open.

The name was inspired by a murder victim.

Baltus Roll, a farmer who lived on the mountain that sits directly behind the Tudor clubhouse at what is now Baltusrol, was a large landowner who traded in apples and other commodities. He was considered wealthy by the standards of 1831. He and his wife, Susannah, lived alone.

At 11 p.m. on the night of February 22, 1831, Roll was awakened by a loud pounding on the door. Two intruders burst into his bedroom and pummeled him before dragging him outside and choking him to death. One of the alleged murderers was captured, and when the other heard about it, he killed himself, apparently with a drug overdose.

Sixty years later, Louis Keller, owner and publisher of the *Social Register*, bought 500 acres of land near Baltus Roll's mountain for the purpose of building a club. A prominent socialite, Miss Louise McAllister, has been credited with coining the name

Baltusrol now had hosted seven U.S. Opens, more than any other club.

5

Baltusrol Golf Club

The fourth hole, par three, 162/194 yards.

The fifth hole, par four, 413 yards.

The sixth hole, par four, 470 yards.

Baltusrol by putting the two names together and dropping the final L.

Thus was born, from death, one of America's most distinguished golf clubs. It is a place the United States Golf Association has designated as the site for 13 national championships, the only club ever to have Open championships on two of its courses — both the Upper Course and the Lower Course — and the club that has hosted more Opens (seven) than any other club.

The Open first came to Baltusrol in 1903. It is one of two clubs from that era remaining on the USGA's more-or-less regular (though unwritten) rota for the national championship. Shinnecock Hills on Long Island is the other, though Shinnecock waited a span of 90 years between Opens, from 1896 to 1986.

The first nine holes at Baltusrol were completed in 1895, the second nine holes were done a year later. On this course, Willie Anderson won the Open and Chandler Egan won the 1904 U.S. Amateur. The course was reworked the year following Egan's win, but it was remodeled to such an extent after that it was a totally different course by 1915 when Jerome Travers became the second amateur to win the U.S. Open.

The membership purchased the golf course from Keller after World War I, and the decision among the swelling ranks was to build another golf course. A.W. Tillinghast was selected as the architect.

The Lower Course, on which the Open has now been contested five times from 1936 to the present, has undergone some changes since then. Robert Trent Jones added more than 500 yards to its overall length in 1954, installing some severe new bunkering and significantly altering the fourth hole, a one-shotter that varies from 162 to 194 yards — most of it carry over a long pond.

One of golf's most delightful anecdotes surrounds that remodeling. It is said that Jones, after the membership had complained that the hole had been made too long and too difficult, went to the tee with a group of members and, with a 4-iron, knocked his tee shot into the hole for an ace.

"Gentlemen," he said, "as you can see, this hole is not too difficult."

The 14th hole, par four, 415 yards.

Baltusrol has needed few defenders through the years. Some holes were lengthened before this Open; and there were other changes as well — the work was done by Jones' son, Rees Jones — but the USGA considered it to be one of the fairest and truest tests of any Open site.

David Eger, the USGA's Senior Director of Rules and Competitions, wrote an article about why the USGA keeps coming back to Baltusrol. Wrote Eger: "The history of the U.S. Open at Baltusrol is a chronicle of dramatic championships, each of them staged with care and efficiency. Fundamentally, Baltusrol is a golf club — not a country club. All of its members know and love the game, and within their club is a century-old culture that has taught them how to deal with both the traditions and travails of the National Open. They know how to make an Open work."

And they know how to maintain tradition. Change comes glacially to Baltusrol. Glitter is not on the agenda. There are members who can recall the day in 1957 when the clubhouse committee approved the playing of recorded music in the dining room. There was an uproar. Music was banned until 1972. There are those who still find it intrusive.

The essence of Baltusrol is not altogether different from what it was back when Keller was rounding up 50 original members and charging $10 a head for dues. The essence is that it is immutable, a link to a simpler time and a place where permanence is palpable, from the creaky wooden floors to the elegant moustache of Bill Eldridge — who has served cocktails in the upstairs lounge since 1941.

There are more than 120 members at Baltusrol who are single-digit handicappers. This would be 12 percent of the membership, a respectable number for such an enclave. The people here are serious about their golf and serious about their golf championships.

This kind of devotion to the game is what makes the membership agreeable to putting up with the many inconveniences of holding an Open. Virtually every great champion in the history of American golf has strolled the grounds at Baltusrol. That's a tradition that should endure.

93rd U. S. Open

The 15th hole, par four, 430 yards.

The 16th hole, par three, 180/216 yards.

93rd U.S. Open
Prologue

No one was quite certain what to expect when the U.S. Open returned to Baltusrol after a 13-year hiatus. Unlike the weeks and months leading up to the last several national championships, there was neither a solid favorite nor a clear-cut theme to frame the proceedings.

Although it seemed only yesterday that Curtis Strange was embarking on his quest for a third straight Open to tie Willie Anderson's record, it was not. In the three intervening seasons, Curtis's game has fallen on lean times and the only talk of three-peat was on the basketball courts of Chicago and Phoenix, where the Bulls were trying to win their third straight NBA title.

There was not even a decent debate over a dominating player on the American front, since no one has come close to dominating. The Masters title was once again in Euro-

Baltusrol greeted the return of the U.S. Open as Tom Kite (opposite page) set out to defend his title.

Prologue

With a win at The Masters this year, Bernhard Langer was certainly a favorite.

Nick Faldo, the No. 1 player in the world, with his caddie, Fanny Sunesson.

pean hands, with Bernhard Langer's convincing victory at Augusta National. The head-to-head duel that raged last year between Fred Couples and Davis Love III going into the Open, where each player had three victories and more than $1 million in earnings before June, had long since petered out. Couples had won just once coming into the Open, at the Honda Classic. Love was winless for 1993 and hadn't really even contended since The Nestle Invitational at Bay Hill, a week after Couples' win, where he finished tied for second.

An amorphous season, though, has a way of crystallizing at the Open. And there was plenty of hope for that. It began with the No. 1 player in the world, Nick Faldo. Certainly, there was much anticipation surrounding the appearance of Faldo at Baltusrol, especially after his pilgrimage to Fort Worth last year to visit Ben Hogan. By all accounts, Faldo and Hogan spent sev-

Paul Azinger (left) and 1991 Open champion Payne Stewart (right) were friendly rivals on the 1993 PGA Tour, with Azinger having the upper hand.

eral very cordial hours together, with the upshot being that the Wee Ice Mon imparted to Faldo a secret for winning the Open.

Faldo was characteristically coy about the meeting. He would, when questioned about Hogan's advice, reply only, "It's a secret and we'll let you know after the Open."

The suspense was ameliorated slightly by Faldo's ho-hum season coming in. He had but one victory early in the season in Singapore at the Johnnie Walker Classic, and had generally been performing in a disinterested fashion. Perhaps the Open would be the tonic to get him going.

Though American golf had been deprived of the Couples and Love show for the better part of 1993, the season had not been without some friendly rivalry between Paul Azinger and Payne Stewart, best of friends and two of the best players on the PGA Tour. Azinger held the upper hand, both in earnings ($747,412 to $665,524) and victories (1-0).

Helping to spice matters up was the way in which Azinger won — by holing an extremely difficult bunker shot at the 72nd hole of the Memorial Tournament to defeat Stewart.

"Paul just made a great shot and I wasn't able to respond to it," said Stewart, who subsequently three-putted from eight feet to finish two shots behind his buddy. "But Payne Stewart will be back."

Emotionally, it took Stewart all of 30 minutes to recover from the defeat. Immediately after his press conference, he went to the locker room and stuffed the toes of Azinger's shoes with sliced bananas. Stewart had the look of someone who could very well make some serious noise coming into the Open. He had finished in the top three five times, with two seconds.

Prologue

"Payne is really playing great," Azinger said. "I wouldn't be at all surprised to see him play well in the Open. He's got his confidence back and he's swinging at it great. Watch out for him at Baltusrol."

This was more than a couple of pals engaging in mutual admiration. Both had seen signs in their own games, and in those of one another, that there could be some good things in the offing for the rest of the season. Their duel down the stretch at the Memorial impressed one of golf's most critical set of eyes, those of tournament host and founder Jack Nicklaus.

"I think what you saw was some marvelous golf down the stretch by both Payne and Paul," Nicklaus said. "They were throwing shots back and forth at each other. It was fun to watch. They're both fine players."

And what of Nicklaus himself? He would be playing in his 37th Open, in on a special exemption from the USGA, and had been working very hard on his game. The last thing Nicklaus wanted to do was embarrass himself. He had not played particularly well at his own tournament, carding a mortifying 81 in the third round, but had been encouraged by his play in a practice round at Baltusrol early in the week.

Fanciful? Well, certainly. Nicklaus, 53, hadn't won on the regular tour since his spectacular 1986 victory at The Masters. For that matter, he hadn't won on the Senior PGA Tour since the 1991 Senior U.S. Open. But there were many who recalled what happened when Jack came to Baltusrol in 1980 after his first winless season and staged his memorable four-day duel with Isao Aoki.

"This golf course holds a lot of positive memories for me," Nicklaus said the week before the tournament. "It's conceivable I could play well."

Greg Norman also had toured the course the week before the Open, and pronounced it the fairest U.S. Open track he had ever seen. His game was in more than fair condition, too. He was leading the PGA Tour in the Vardon Trophy race with a stroke average of 69.59, had one victory, a second and two fourths in eight events and was driving the ball particularly well.

On a golf course that put the driver back in the player's hands, and one that was extremely long, Norman definitely looked like a player to watch.

There even was some sentiment for Seve Ballesteros, whose unrequited love affair with the major he seems destined not to win was heightened by his return to the site of his starting-time blunder in 1980. It was at Baltusrol that Ballesteros had been caught in traffic and missed his starting time

Vijay Singh had emerged as Fiji's first world-class golfer and won at Westchester.

Davis Love III hadn't kept his 1992 pace.

13 years ago. Perhaps the golf course owed him one. At least one American player thought so. When he saw the relatively sparse rough and the mowed areas around the front of the greens that allowed bump-and-run shots, Billy Andrade declared, "This is the year Seve Ballesteros finally wins the U.S. Open."

There were some young American pros who might have something to say about that. Andrade, who grew up nearby in Rhode Island, was one of them. So was Lee Janzen, 28, of whom Tom Watson had said earlier in the year, "I like the way Lee Janzen plays golf."

Baltusrol seemed as good a place as any for an amorphous season to take shape. As straightforward as any golf course on the unofficial U.S. Open rota, it would provide the complete examination of a player's game and some straight answers about who was on top of it.

Jack Nicklaus had won the 1980 U.S. Open, and two of his four Open titles, at Baltusrol.

93rd U.S. Open
First Round

U.S. Open Thursday, 1993, dawned clear and bright over the New York/New Jersey metropolitan area. The day was windless and warm, a bluebird day. It was a cinch that telephone lines into Wall Street were jammed with calls — from brokers phoning in sick to play hooky.

And why not? The national championship of golf hadn't been contested in the area since the 1986 U.S. Open at Shinnecock Hills on Long Island, and golf fans ravenous to see the greatest players in the world were streaming across the Hudson River into Jersey. Roads leading to Baltusrol were jammed. *The New York Times* called it "The Mother of All Traffic Jams," but for both Jerseyites and New Yorkers, who have grown used to such inconveniences, a seven-year wait to see the Open was worth whatever delays traffic produced.

This truly was an Open for the ages — not to mention the aged. Jack Nicklaus, 53, returned to the site of two of his four Open titles as the oldest player in the field. And the appearance on the national scene of Ted Oh, 16, a high school sophomore from Torrance, California, was the other end of the spectrum. Subplots abounded, such as:

Could Bernhard Langer, the Masters champion, overcome the stiff neck that had kept him from practicing on the eve of the Open? Would Fred Couples break out of

Joey Sindelar (opposite page) became the first to share the first-round lead then miss the 36-hole cut. Others with 66s in the first round were Craig Parry (above left) and Scott Hoch (above right).

First Round

Greg Norman had an unspectacular 73.

yards, but not many.

A light rainy season also had produced a thinner, wispier rough than is customary at most U.S. Open sites. The primary rough was still five inches high, and the six-foot swaths of intermediate rough were still at one and a half inches, but the ball could be advanced from the rough. Generally, the cost of hitting the rough in a U.S. Open is half a stroke. In the first round, it was .36 or about one-third of a stroke. That might seem minute, but it made a large difference.

By the end of the day, the average score — 72.282 — was the lowest ever for a first round in the Open, surpassing the previous mark of 73.402 set at Oak Hill Country Club in Rochester, New York, in 1989. When his lethargy and win an Open at a site that seemed to suit his strength — length? Could Tom Watson, at age 43, get back into the major championship picture now that a decade has passed since his last major victory?

Could John Daly hit the green at the 630-yard 17th hole in two shots, something no one had ever done? And would heavy traffic cause a repeat of the infamous 1980 Baltusrol incident where Seve Ballesteros missed his tee time and was disqualified?

The Lower Course at Baltusrol was set up by the USGA with the idea of putting the driver back in the hands of the players. The pros welcomed it. "I'll use driver all week," said Mark McCumber. "They've set it up so you can drive the golf ball. They've put that club back in play."

Landing areas in most of the 14 fairways were 35 yards across. There were spots where the fairway widths narrowed to 28

Lee Janzen, with 67, was just behind the leaders, tied with Craig Stadler (opposite page), who had a new putter.

more than a stroke is cut off the previous low for a field stroke average, it has to be attributable to a combination of factors.

Many of the greens were open in the front, giving players the option of playing fliers short of the putting surfaces and running them into the pins. Couples did just this on the first hole, a 470-yard par four. He drove the ball in the primary rough to the right, but hit a flier with a 7-iron and rolled his ball onto the putting surface. Shots like this were part of the reason why not a disparaging word was heard from the players about the way the course was set up by David Eger, the USGA's Senior Director of Rules and Competitions.

The players took to the task with gusto.

First Round

Scott Hoch	66	-4
Joey Sindelar	66	-4
Craig Parry	66	-4
Lee Janzen	67	-3
Craig Stadler	67	-3
Mike Smith	68	-2
Corey Pavin	68	-2
Fred Couples	68	-2
Robert Wrenn	68	-2
Blaine McCallister	68	-2
Rocco Mediate	68	-2
Raymond Floyd	68	-2

The light rough improved Fred Couples' chances to score well. He opened with 68.

Before long, red numbers started dotting the leaderboards. It's not often easier to drive in the U.S. Open than it is on the interstate, but that was the situation. And the results weren't long in coming. Three rounds of 66, four under par, were put up by an unlikely trio of leaders.

Scott Hoch was the first player to come in with 66. A 37-year-old veteran coming off a poor season following shoulder surgery, Hoch is no stranger to major championship adventures. He is best remembered for the two-and-a-half-foot putt he missed on the first playoff hole with Nick Faldo at the 1989 Masters Tournament. Faldo went on to win, and though Hoch later won at Las Vegas on the PGA Tour that year, he has since been in eclipse. Except for challenges at Hazeltine, where he finished alone in sixth, Hoch had not been a factor.

Hoch, who had missed the cut in two of his last three tournaments coming into the Open, had a feeling he wasn't long for the lead. He had a mediocre ball-striking day, and birdies at the two par-five finishing holes made his score look better than he had played. "My round today I compare to a duck," he said. "On the surface he looks fine, like he's moving right along, no problems at all. But underneath, he's paddling like heck just to keep up. That's what I felt inside. I had a band-aid on my swing all day."

Joey Sindelar was another unexpected leader. He had come on with a run that began at the 11th, with birdies on four of five holes. A 10-year veteran of the PGA Tour, Sindelar, 35, also had not been playing well coming into the Open. Two months earlier, in a pro-am at the Kemper Open, he had been beaten by his playing partner — former Vice President Dan Quayle — by four strokes.

"This was not a particularly good round from tee to green," Sindelar said, "but it was a functional round. The scoring conditions were as good as you could have for a U.S. Open Championship and that has to do with the course setup and the weather. For a classic, tough, great test of golf on a nice golf day, this is as good as it gets."

Craig Parry, the Australian who is known as "Popeye" for his large forearms, was the third player to shoot 66. Parry also is known more for his major championship misfortune than success. He led The Masters through three rounds in 1992, but shot 78 in the fourth round and finished tied for 13th.

1986 Open champion Raymond Floyd was among seven with 68s.

Corey Pavin, with two second-place finishes in 1993, was rarely in trouble in the first round.

First Round

Jack Nicklaus, with 70, excited the crowd in the first round.

"I've had a pretty lean 12 months since Augusta last year," said the 26-year-old Parry, who worked the week before the Open with his swing coach, David Leadbetter. "But I'm back hitting the ball solid, working it right to left in addition to left to right."

Young Ted Oh found out all about a different sort of left to right. He played the front nine in 35, one over par, and was charged up on the 10th tee after a birdie at the ninth hole. But he pulled his drive into the left rough and then chopped his ball across the fairway into the right rough. He couldn't hit the green from there, and when he finally got home, he three-putted for a triple bogey.

"I'm 16 years old," Oh said. "I got mad." But he didn't embarrass himself. He shot 76, a very respectable score for the youngest amateur to qualify for the Open since Tyrell Garth, Jr., did so at the age of 14 in 1941.

While all of this was going on, a curly-haired young man was quietly making his fifth birdie of the day, chipping to two feet at the 18th hole and holing the putt to close out with 67. The young man's name was Lee Janzen. His gallery was not large, but his game was. He came into the Open on the heels of a tie for third place the week before at Westchester.

"Last week was similar to U.S. Open conditions, with high rough and hard, fast greens," Janzen said. "I don't want to say that because of last week that I have to play well here, but there could be something to that."

Yes, there could. But there were three more rigorous days ahead, and there were 138 players sitting within 10 strokes of the lead, and no one was looking very hard at Lee Janzen, who was tied with Craig Stadler for fourth place. There were Couples and Raymond Floyd at 68 to consider. Rocco Mediate, once Janzen's teammate at Florida

Southern, also was at 68, as were Corey Pavin, Mike Smith, Robert Wrenn and Blaine McCallister.

Nicklaus somehow managed to shoot 70, and there was tremendous excitement over U.S. Amateur champion Justin Leonard, who had played with Faldo and defending champion Tom Kite and had beaten both of them with a round of 69, birdieing the last hole.

Langer somehow managed to struggle through his round, shooting 74. Langer had to take anti-inflammatory drugs and became woozy during play. At the sixth hole, he opened his umbrella to shade himself from the sun and was so disoriented that he considered walking off.

"I couldn't tell where I was aiming or what I was doing," he said. After making double bogey at the hole, Langer pulled himself together and finished the round.

Daly didn't make the green at No. 17 because his drive found the left rough. But there would be more tries. For a golf course that one national golf publication labeled "The Longest Yawn," Baltusrol was providing an awful lot of excitement. Greg Norman, one of golf's most stimulating players, got off to an unspectacular start with 73, but Watson, who shot 70 and was off to his best Open start since 1981 — was quick to point something out.

"This is the U.S. Open and you can still be in it if you shoot four or five over par if you can come back," he said. "You put 66 with 75 and you're right back in it."

With a triple bogey, 16-year-old Ted Oh shot 76.

Under medication, Bernhard Langer shot 74.

93rd U.S. Open
Second Round

Friday was supposed to be the day the stars came out and the upstarts packed it in. Only half of that supposition was correct.

The stars definitely came out. Their names were Tom Watson, Payne Stewart and Nick Price. Also Corey Pavin and Fred Couples. Big names with games to match. The illustrious threesome of Watson, Stewart and Price, a trio that collectively holds 11 Grand Slam titles, all shot rounds of 66. Packed in like a sleeve of balls, they positioned themselves for the weekend war of attrition that the U.S. Open usually becomes.

And bursting into the picture was John Daly, exploding onto the leaderboard the way John Madden used to tear through the props onto the set of those old television commercials — "And another thing …!" Going where no golfer has gone before, in just about everything imaginable, has been Daly's leitmotif since he first muscled his way into everyone's consciousness with his fanciful win at the 1991 PGA Championship.

The Open might seem like an impossible dream for Daly, 27, but this time he at least reached the unreachable green. He went 630

Tom Watson (opposite page) had a good spring, and was determined to continue playing well.

Lee Janzen was in unfamiliar territory.

yards in two shots at the 17th hole. Uphill. But more on that later.

Because Daly was only a bright sidelight to the real goings on. In the midst of it all — all the fireworks and hoopla and Daly whoops and roars that rolled across the historic course below Watchung Mountain — one man strolled along without a trace of stress on his baby-faced countenance.

And he was the real story. The one surprise who didn't go away, Lee Janzen, added another 67 to his first. The kid from Kissimmee, Florida, a two-time winner on the PGA Tour but largely unrecognized by anyone but members of the golf cognoscenti, had put himself in some ultrafast company. And we're not just talking about Watson and Stewart, who trailed him by two strokes after their 66s. We're not just talking about Price, who was another stroke back, or Pavin, also three strokes back after 69 to go with his opening 68.

We're talking about Jack Nicklaus. Janzen's 134 tied the 36-hole record set by Nicklaus (and equaled in 1985 by Chen Tze-Chung) right here at Baltusrol in 1980.

Lee Janzen, taming the same course as Jack Nicklaus, with the same score Nicklaus had? Sure, and under very similar conditions. The greens were just as fast and the rough was just as high, though not as thick as in 1980. Janzen, however, labored under no delusions.

"I feel like I have a long, long way to go to be one of the great players," Janzen said. "I've matured. I've improved quite a bit. My game is getting better. But I don't feel like I'm at a level with these guys quite yet."

And he knows the notion of ever attaining Nicklaus levels is just about implausible. But his play over the first two days showed just how good a player Janzen is and underscored the fact that the man who had won twice in the desert was more than ready for a leading role just across the Hudson from the Great White Way.

On Thursday, he missed just two fairways. His putter was hotter than the concrete around Newark Airport. He took 27 putts in the first round and 28 in the second. The only player among the leaders who approached those kind of putting stats was Watson, who followed Thursday's 29 putts with 28 on Friday.

Watson's putting and his ongoing battle with the yips were a topic of Friday conversation. He missed a three-and-a-half-footer for par at the second hole and promptly gave himself a stern lecture. Then, there were the 10 putts Watson took on the sixth green.

They were just practice putts, but they caused quite a stir. Watson, who had taken 12 putts in the first six holes, was unhappy with the way he was rolling the ball. He walked over to USGA rules official Ken Lindsey and asked if it would be acceptable to take a few practice putts, since the players in the group behind — Grant Waite, Mike Donald and Massy Kuramoto — were not yet ready to hit into the green.

"Absolutely," Lindsey replied.

So Watson worked on his stroke, with caddie Bruce Edwards flipping the ball back after each stroke. He opened his shoulders slightly to get through the ball and with each stroke it started to feel better.

"We're not allowed to do that on Tour and you can't do it here if there's somebody waiting to hit to the green," Watson said. "But we had nobody waiting and where we were going to have to wait on the next tee anyway, I had the luxury of hitting a few practice putts. It seemed to work."

It certainly did. Watson required just 16 putts over the next 12 holes. Still, he was not slam-dunking the three- and four-footers the way he did in his heyday. He was judging the longer putts quite well — he holed two 20-footers for birdies — and sort of squeezing the shorter ones into the hole. The yips were still shadowing him like a bad debt.

And Stewart was stalking everyone like a debt collector. Denied victory since beating Scott Simpson in the 1991 U.S. Open playoff at Hazeltine, Stewart was playing the most consistent, if frustrating, golf of anyone anywhere in the world. Six times already in 1993 he had been among the top six. He had two second-place finishes and was robbed of victory by Paul Azinger's bunker shot on the 72nd hole of the Memorial Tournament just two weeks before.

Payne's play had been almost flawless. Only a three-putt bogey from 50 feet at the 17th hole marred his five-birdie round. He had reworked his alignment on the practice tee following his opening round, and was going at the ball with extreme confidence and excellent tempo.

"The difference for me has been night and day," Stewart said. "I got away with the round on Thursday not being comfortable. Now I'm comfortable again and I'm hitting the ball the way I have been all year."

When Stewart is focused, you could set a bomb off next to his foot and get only a raised eyebrow. He was playing in the threesome with Daly, and got a first-hand look at the monumental achievement of golf's Paul Bunyan. He claimed not to notice.

"What'd he do?" Stewart said.

Everyone else at Baltusrol knew. Each

Awesome John Daly (opposite page) shown here driving off the 17th tee, as he became the first to reach that green in two strokes.

Second Round

Payne Stewart's play was almost flawless.

John Cook rebounded from 75 to 66.

day, both in practice and during the tournament, the marshals and spectators at the 17th tee had been extorting Daly to do it. "You gonna do it today, John?" one of them asked as he stepped through the ropes and onto the tee. "Gonna try. Gonna try," Daly said.

Now, history holds that this green had never been hit in two shots. That isn't precisely true. In the 1967 Open, the assistant pro at Baltusrol, Billy Farrell, also hit the 17th in two shots. But there was a big difference. First, the tees were up, making the hole measure somewhere in the 570-yard range. Second, Farrell took a short cut unavailable to current players. He hit his tee shot into the 17th fairway at the Upper Course. That was the corporate tent village this week. His second shot was downhill, about 232 yards, and he used a 3-wood to get home.

"Look," said Farrell, who has spent the last 26 years as the head pro at Stanwich Club in Greenwich, Connecticut, "there isn't anybody who's as long as John Daly."

No question about that. Daly bombed his tee shot 325 yards with a draw, and it came to rest a few yards from the first cut of left rough. It could not have been placed better. His earlier attempts at the hole had wound up in the rough to the left. Now he had a chance. From that spot, he had 282 yards to the front of the green, 287 yards to the pin. He took out a 1-iron. He does not carry a 3-wood, since he has no need for one.

What happened next was one of those rare sports moments. Daly's 1-iron shot started out high and hard. He leaped at it so powerfully, he finished out of balance. The ball landed in the rough in front of the green, but was so hot it kept on going, bounding to the fringe and trundling onto the green, eventually stopping some 45 feet past the hole. The shot was all uphill.

It was electrifying. Dave Anderson of *The New York Times* described the roar as sounding "like the roars that once responded to a moonshot home run by Mickey Mantle or Reggie Jackson ... a roar of awe at how far John Daly hits a golf ball."

Second Round

Lee Janzen	67-67—134	-6
Tom Watson	70-66—136	-4
Payne Stewart	70-66—136	-4
Nick Price	71-66—137	-3
Corey Pavin	68-69—137	-3
Scott Hoch	66-72—138	-2
Paul Azinger	71-68—139	-1
Billy Andrade	72-67—139	-1
Mike Standly	70-69—139	-1
Fred Couples	68-71—139	-1
Jeff Maggert	69-70—139	-1
Bob Gilder	70-69—139	-1

Scott Hoch, with 72, fared best among the first-round leaders.

It was a Friday of firsts. Janzen tying the scoring record, Daly hitting the 17th green, Joey Sindelar becoming the first player ever to lead or share the lead in the first round and then miss the cut (he went 66-79), the

Paul Azinger was in good position at 139.

Nick Price posted one of the four 66s.

Second Round

  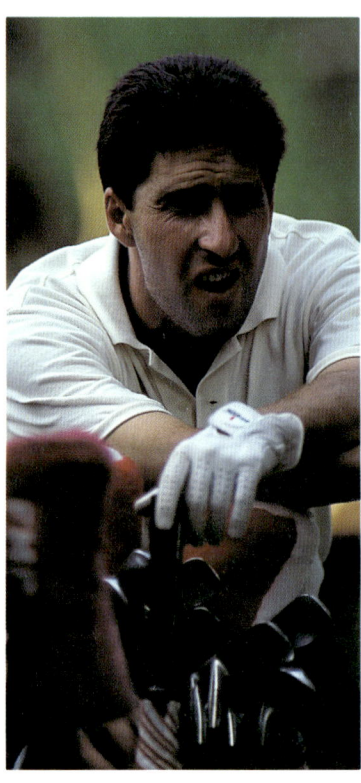

Among the prominent players missing the 36-hole cut were Tom Kite (left), Seve Ballesteros (center) and Jose Maria Olazabal (right).

USGA officials relied as usual on the Stimpmeter to measure the speed of the greens.

first time 88 players have ever made the cut (the additional 27 payout spots cost the USGA $143,964) and the first time Janzen had made the cut in four Open tries.

This time, Janzen not only had made the cut (which this year was at 144), but he had eliminated several big-name players that were not within 10 shots of the standard he set. Casualties included defending champion Tom Kite, whose second round 70 could not offset his opening 75. And Langer who, despite his game effort, could not overcome his stiff neck. His 71 left him at 145 and he thus became the first reigning Masters champion to miss the cut at the Open since he himself did it back in 1985.

International stars were sent packing of their own accord. Greg Norman, who could never get comfortable on the subtle putting surfaces and was having problems concen-

Nick Faldo, at 144, barely made the 36-hole cut.

trating, shot 147. Seve Ballesteros and Jose Maria Olazabal shot identical 148s and it was *adios* once again to the charismatic Spaniards. Vijay Singh of Fiji, who had stunned the metropolitan area with his victory the week before at Westchester, missed his first cut of the year on any continent, shooting 145 that took everyone by surprise.

The hot, muggy weekend loomed with the prospect of just about anything. No scenario was too fanciful. Even Jack Nicklaus, who had followed his opening-round 70 with 72, was not out of the question.

"I don't see any reason why I can't," Nicklaus said when asked if he could possibly pull it off.

Neither did anyone else. Maybe it was the heat. Then, again, maybe it was just the Open.

Billy Andrade's 67 provided a 139 total.

93rd U.S. Open
Third Round

The heat is always on in the last two rounds of the U.S. Open. But on Saturday, it wasn't just Open pressure that was making the competitors drip sweat. It was the dreaded heat and humidity that gripped the metropolitan area like a chain-mail glove.

As the sun rose higher, so did the temperatures, right up to a flesh-melting 102 degrees. While the leaders prepared to tee off, the cauldron began to bubble with possibilities.

Among them was the potential for a run by the U.S. Amateur champion, Justin Leonard, who was playing like a professional. He began the day at even par, just six strokes behind Lee Janzen and four behind the second-place tandem of Payne Stewart and Tom Watson.

Leonard had played two days with defending champion Tom Kite and Nick Faldo, and had beaten them both. Kite missed the 36-hole cut and Faldo already had finished his Saturday round of 73 before Leonard even teed off at 12:29 p.m., just nine groups in front of the leaders.

"I think an amateur can win a major championship," Leonard said. "I'm not saying that I can or will. But what I'm saying is an amateur can win a major somewhere down the line."

Then there was the prospect of a true comeback by Watson, who was teeing off in the last Open pairing on Saturday for the first time since 1987. Could it be that Watson, without a victory in a major since the 1983 British Open, was really on the verge of stepping back into the throne room?

Paul Azinger was lurking at one under par, Scott Hoch had hung tough at two under, and Corey Pavin, for whom many believed Baltusrol was simply too long a golf course, was right there at three under par.

Justin Leonard was well among the leaders.

Those who were anticipating a Saturday charge by Fred Couples got an early indicator of what was to come. Couples went through his unorthodox loosening-up ritual on the first tee — taking as many swings left-handed as he did right-handed — and then put a massive left-to-left pull swing on his opening tee shot. The ball went through the fence bordering the property, nearly to Shunpike Road, and Couples had to take the long walk back to the tee. He made double bogey. Though he fought his way to a one-over-par 71, he was not a factor again.

Lee Janzen (opposite page) endured the humidity, heat and pressure of the U.S. Open.

Mike Donald shot 67, one of his few highlights since the 1990 Open.

Fred Couples didn't figure after driving out of bounds at No. 1.

That opening hole, a daunting 470-yard par four that is straighter than the center line on a highway, usually set the tone for the day. Mike Donald was playing the hole at about 9:25 in the morning, and found himself some 30 yards short of the green in two strokes. He then pitched in for birdie and wound up shooting 67, tying for the second-lowest score of the day. With that, he leaped over 60 players, from a tie for 72nd place to a tie for 12th.

Donald, best remembered for his near-miss at the 1990 U.S. Open at Medinah, where he lost a playoff to Hale Irwin, was back in the thick of things at the Open. He had played his way into the field as the medalist in his sectional qualifier and now he was at least in position for a shot at the top 15 after going around Baltusrol without a bogey.

"It wasn't a Hogan-type round," said Donald, who missed five fairways and hit

Birdies on Nos. 13 and 15 kept Payne Stewart (opposite page) in pursuit of the title.

11 greens. "But anytime you can go around a U.S. Open course without any bogeys, you're happy. I'm not going to lose much ground sitting here in the clubhouse."

He was right about that. Although the golf course was still in a fairly generous mood, there was not much movement. Only 18 players would break par, and the man who began the day with the lead held it when the day was done.

Janzen started the day like he was intent on blowing the field away. He birdied the first hole, hitting driver and 7-iron to six feet and making the putt. He was not at all unnerved by being paired with Watson. He split the fairway at the second hole with a 2-iron off the tee and then hit his 7-iron approach two feet away, holing that to go eight under par.

The kid looked cool. He was now four strokes clear of the field. If anything, it was Watson who seemed a little uncomfortable with his game. He missed a three-footer at the third hole and, after a spectacular birdie at the fourth, where he nearly holed his 6-

Third Round

iron shot, knocking it four inches from the hole, he bogeyed the fifth and missed a four-footer at the seventh for another bogey.

"I had a couple of twitches out there," said Watson, who missed a four-footer at the 12th and bogeyed the last hole for 73 that pushed him into a tie for sixth place with six others at one under par. One of the players in that group was Fred Funk, who was paired with Jack Nicklaus when the day started and who leaped over half the field with his round of 67.

Janzen couldn't maintain the fast start. He bogeyed the third and fifth holes and had to make a 10-footer for par at the sixth. His lead was still two strokes over Watson at this point, and he settled down with a birdie at the ninth and a good save at the 11th. No one was really making a move. At least not yet.

Creeping along in his major championship mode of one par after another was Stewart, who reeled off 12 straight pars. His only makeable putts were at the second hole, where he missed from 12 feet, and the 12th, where he missed from 15 feet. Like everyone in the field, Stewart was fighting the sly breaks that were designed into the greens by the original architect, A.W. Tillinghast. These greens and their critical subtleties were really the last line of defense against the pros. Stewart's friend and fellow competitor Paul Azinger had spent two days trying to solve the mysteries of the greens.

Craig Parry turned away in anguish after this chip shot at No. 6.

Third Round

Lee Janzen	67-67-69—203	-7
Payne Stewart	70-66-68—204	-6
Nick Price	71-66-70—207	-3
David Edwards	70-72-66—208	-2
Paul Azinger	71-68-69—208	-2
Fred Funk	70-72-67—209	-1
John Adams	70-70-69—209	-1
Craig Parry	66-74-69—209	-1
Wayne Levi	71-69-69—209	-1
Mike Standly	70-69-70—209	-1
Tom Watson	70-66-73—209	-1

"I missed nine putts in the five-to-seven-foot range the first two days," Azinger said. "It seemed like every time I had one that length, I missed it. But in today's round I didn't miss one."

Whatever it was that Azinger saw, it worked. He shot 69 and was in fourth place, tied with David Edwards at two under par, going into the final day. Edwards, too, had solved the greens, jumping into the fray with 66, the day's lowest round, fashioned by an otherworldly 25 putts, the fewest putts anyone took all week.

Stewart broke away from the pack and right onto Janzen's back with two birdies coming in. He made a two-footer at the 13th hole and two-putted from 35 feet at the 18th after hitting the green in two shots, driver

Nick Price thought this putt at No. 6 was in the hole — but it slid away.

Third Round

Paul Azinger, tied for fourth place, was pleased by his putting.

A 66 put David Edwards in contention.

and 5-iron. When he finally made the birdie at the 13th, he put his ball in his mouth so he could have his hands free to applaud himself. There was no mistaking the way the 1991 Open champion was playing.

He had the lean and hungry look.

"I did what I wanted to do today," Stewart said. "I drove the ball in the fairway and gave myself a chance. I feel confident in this position. I'm used to it. I have given myself an opportunity to win."

And he wasn't alone. Nick Price also was right there. He might have been even closer if he had been able to make any putts at all. To get an idea of how well Price was striking it, all you have to know is that he hit 16 greens and shot even par. He took 34 putts.

"When you hit the ball well and don't make any score, it's the most frustrating

Fred Funk shot 67 to share sixth place at one under par.

Nolan Henke was at even par and tied for 12th place after his 67.

thing in golf," Price said. "But I figure it will work out sooner or later. The thing with this game is that you have to persevere."

That could have been Janzen's motto, because that's exactly what he did. He kept his head and his putting stroke at the 15th hole, and made a great bogey when a double bogey seemed likely. Often, it is not the spectacular birdie or eagle that keeps a player on track in the Open. It is the save, either for par or, in this case, for bogey.

Janzen left his 7-iron approach shot on the 15th hole short of the green. It was a poor shot from the fairway, but he was left with a reasonably easy chip. He hit it too hard, and the shot went through the green. His fourth shot was a chip that ran 10 feet past the hole. If he were to miss the putt coming back, he would fall to five under par for the championship and into a tie with Stewart.

He poured the putt right in the middle of the hole. Then he birdied the last hole for good measure, right after Stewart had done the same. Lee Janzen now had tied the 54-

Tom Watson fell back with his 73.

Third Round

hole Open record at 203, sharing it with Chen Tze-Chung (Oakland Hills in 1985) and George Burns (Merion in 1981) and had shot his third straight round in the 60s. People were starting to look at him differently.

Like, who is this kid in the baseball-style hat with the baby face and the nerves of a hit man?

"Well, he's entering new territory tomorrow," said Price. "That's stating the obvious, but having never been in the lead of a major championship going into the last round is something that's a little different. But he is very capable of winning this championship. I've played a lot with him. He's an extremely intelligent golfer. He plays well within his capabilities. He's an exceptionally good putter. I don't see him fading at all."

None of the talk seemed to mean anything to Janzen. That expression of his, eerily implacable and inscrutable, hadn't changed. He was here to do his best, he said. He wasn't going to talk about winning or finishing in the top 10 or caving in like papier-mâché.

"It's very early in my career for majors," he said. "I haven't played in too many. I'm very pleased to be in the lead. I'm going to take tomorrow as just one round, and I'm going to play the best I can."

He would find out soon enough if that would be good enough.

Fuzzy Zoeller (left) and John Daly were a popular pairing, although neither challenged the leaders.

The warning signs went up, but weather did not interfere with the third round.

Each day the tees were re-sodded to provide perfect practice conditions.

93rd U.S. Open
Fourth Round

In the depths of the huge Tudor clubhouse at Baltusrol, Lee Janzen walked down a corridor from the locker room toward a door leading to the practice green. It was U.S. Open Sunday, and he was leading. In his hand was his putter. He carried it like a sword, like Excalibur.

He walked past a photo exhibit of Open champions past. There were photographs of Jack Nicklaus. One was the famous shot of Jack holding his putter high in his left hand after making the critical putt at the 71st hole in 1980. There were photographs of a young Nicklaus in 1967, his powerful legs and shoulders working as one in the patented takeaway.

Someone had put together a collage of past winners at Baltusrol and it stood on an easel. Willie Anderson, 1903; Jerome Travers, 1915; Tony Manero, 1936; Ed Furgol, 1954; Jack Nicklaus, 1967 and 1980. There was a blank circle in the middle over the heading "1993 Winner." As he walked by, Lee Janzen's face was reflected in the transparent acrylic plastic covering the pictures. Actually, his profile was reflected.

The duel between Payne Stewart and Lee Janzen was virtually settled when Janzen holed this chip at No. 16 from 30 feet to take a two-stroke lead.

Fourth Round

Despite two early birdies, Paul Azinger did not mount a threat.

Craig Parry shot 68 to tie Azinger for third place, five strokes behind.

Because he did not turn to look.

Straight down the hall and through the door, wordlessly, Janzen walked out into the bright, hot day.

"More than anyone I know," said Janzen's long-time teacher, Rick Smith, "Lee lives in the here and now. He won't get caught up in what happened and he won't get caught up in what might happen. He thinks about what is."

In the past decade, only two 54-hole leaders had won the U.S. Open, Curtis Strange in 1989 and Payne Stewart in 1991. Both needed Monday playoffs. Here was Lee Janzen, 28, who had missed the cut in his three previous U.S. Open appearances, trying to join that fraternity. And then there was the question of the photo grouping in the hallway of the clubhouse.

This would be enough to make most young players lose their lunch. The question now would be whether Janzen was most young players or *the* young player, the one who is to emerge from the twenty-

Tom Watson's 69 tied for fifth place.

With two 69s, Jeff Sluman tied for 11th place.

something set and become something more than just a chaser of checks and winner of minors.

Janzen had essentially five things between him and the U.S. Open title. He had Payne Stewart, one shot back at six under par and very, very confident. He had Nick Price, four shots back at three under par and hitting the ball as well as anyone in the tournament. He had Paul Azinger, starting the day at two under, five back, and — having figured out the subtleties of the greens — very capable of making a run. He had Tom Watson and all that history, six back.

And he had himself.

He would need to slay them all, and he was holding one of the weapons he would use as he walked out of the clubhouse. There was one other club in his bag that he would need to inflict the coup de grâce. For now, he had just one thought at the first tee.

"Just make a good swing and hit it in the fairway," he recalled.

Which he did. The first-tee scene was illuminated by an opaque light diffused by gray clouds. There was not a breath of wind. Janzen struck his tee shot true. He was off. He made an excellent par save from the bunker at the hole, and Stewart stumbled, making bogey after spraying his approach shot right of the green and failing to get up and down, missing an eight-footer.

Azinger and Watson both had bogeyed the first hole. Azinger then leaped back into the picture at three under par with consecutive birdies at the second and third holes. Watson, though, went away with a double bogey at the second. He would fight back bravely, shoot 69 and tie for fifth, but that double effectively ended his Open bid.

A birdie at the third and a bogey at the seventh and Janzen made the turn with only Stewart, on him like Velcro, still with a chance, one shot behind. Azinger was back to one under par after consecutive bogeys at the sixth and seventh holes, and he would

45

Fourth Round

Fourth Round

Lee Janzen	67-67-69-69—272	-8
Payne Stewart	70-66-68-70—274	-6
Craig Parry	66-74-69-68—277	-3
Paul Azinger	71-68-69-69—277	-3
Scott Hoch	66-72-72-68—278	-2
Tom Watson	70-66-73-69—278	-2
Ernie Els	71-73-68-67—279	-1
Raymond Floyd	68-73-70-68—279	-1
Nolan Henke	72-71-67-69—279	-1
Fred Funk	70-72-67-70—279	-1

South Africa's Ernie Els tied for seventh place.

Raymond Floyd closed with 68.

not contend, eventually finishing tied for third with Craig Parry. Stewart and Janzen had nine holes left.

It was at the 10th hole that people started thinking about things like destiny or, at the very least, some intervention by the ghost of Baltus Roll himself.

It was here that Janzen hit the shot that defied physics as we know it, when his golf ball seemed to go right through the trunk of one of the fattest oaks in the forest. He had pushed his drive and was trying to hit a 5-iron shot over the tree. The ball took off low off the face, and Janzen figured he was dead.

"I'm thinking, 'Well, that's probably going to bounce deeper into the trees and I'm going to make double bogey. Better bear

In his Sunday red, Curtis Strange finished strong with 67.

Nick Price slipped to 73 and was eight back.

Fourth Round

A 20-foot birdie at No. 9 brought Payne Stewart within one stroke.

down on these last eight holes,'" Janzen said later.

But no. The ball disappeared, through the limbs and the leaves and landed right on the green. "Huge break," Janzen said. How about otherworldly break? When Janzen two-putted for par, Stewart must have felt like someone punched him in the solar plexus.

And there would be more to come right after he caught his breath.

Because Janzen missed a five-footer at the 12th hole. At that point, even with the breaks, he was two over par for the day. Now he was tied with Stewart at five under and the entire U.S. Open would come down to the last six holes. He was starting to feel slightly fatigued, a combination of the heat and the suffocating pressure.

Then at the 14th hole, another second wind. Stewart missed the fairway to the right and put his approach shot into the greenside bunker. Janzen hit his drive in the fairway and then hit a beautiful pitch-

Stewart, a true competitor's anguish etched on his face, missed this birdie putt at No. 15, remaining one behind Lee Janzen.

ing wedge approach that bounced on the green and curled within 15 feet of the cup. He put one of his best strokes on the putt, and it went into the center of the hole for a one-stroke lead.

"I felt like a different person after that," Janzen said. "I had felt tired. I was struggling. That putt gave me the energy to keep going."

Drawing on that energy two holes later, Janzen holed the biggest shot of the Open. It was the defining moment of this championship, just as Tom Watson's holed wedge shot at the 71st hole of the 1982 Open, the one that secured his lone U.S. Open victory and denied Jack Nicklaus his last, was the singular stroke in that historic encounter.

Janzen's tee shot at the 204-yard 16th hole fell 30 feet short and left of the cup, in the tall grass. He had a good lie. The clarity that had entered his mind after the birdie at the 14th told him this chip was makable. Stewart was on the green, but farther away, perhaps 45 feet. Stewart said to Janzen, "What would you like to do?" Janzen, aware that the momentum swing would be huge if he holed the chip, replied, "Whatever you want to do." Stewart said, "Come up if you want to." Again, Janzen replied, "Whatever you want to do."

Stewart motioned him to go ahead. Later, Janzen would recount that he asked Stewart twice because he wanted to be sure Stewart was comfortable with the decision to let him go first.

Standing near the ropes, watching it all, was Rocco Mediate, Janzen's college teammate when the two were at Florida Southern. He turned to the USGA official next to him. "This is a Watson-type chip," he said.

Sitting in the press tent, two par-five holes and a world away, Tom Watson was about to talk about his round when a huge roar went up. Janzen had holed the chip. Watson was incredulous. "Let's see that!" he said, scrambling down from behind the microphone and over to one of the television monitors. The downhill chip cleared the collar and began to roll like a putt. Near the hole it took a hard break, left to right,

Lee Janzen celebrated his chip-in to take a two-stroke lead with two holes to play.

and disappeared.

Eleven years ago, on the television at his parents' home, Lee Janzen had watched Tom Watson chip in on Jack Nicklaus. He had leaped in the air and nearly put his fingers in the whirring blades of the ceiling fan. Now Watson watched.

Remind him of anything? "Slightly," Watson said, smiling at the memory. "Actually, very poignantly."

As powerful and poignant as the moment was, the Open was not yet over. The two par-five holes lay ahead, and Stewart knew he still had a chance. After the 17th hole, though, he must have wondered. Janzen's drive was headed for forest primeval territory to the right when it smacked a tree and bounced back into the fairway. Destiny's child made par. So did Stewart. At the 18th, Janzen again pushed his tee shot to the right, and it landed in the rough.

Stewart was in the fairway, but his attempt to hit the green with his 3-iron fell just short in the front bunker. Janzen was left with a decision. Should he hit the 7-iron he had in his hand and risk dumping it in the creek that bisected the fairway? Or should he lay up with a sand wedge and risk a shot with a long iron into the green with the Open riding on it?

He chose the sand wedge.

"I knew if I hit it in the water it would've been the dumbest decision in the history of golf," he said.

Lee Janzen (opposite page) holed an eight-foot birdie to wrap up the championship.

Payne Stewart offered his congratulations to the new U.S. Open champion.

So he had a 4-iron in, 192 yards, uphill. After all the work, it came down to this. Stewart could hole out for eagle or, barring that, he could certainly make birdie. The lead was two strokes. If Janzen mishit the shot, he could be in trouble. He pushed it, ever so slightly. But the ball underwent some magic in flight correction. It bounced in the fringe and then somehow kicked left. Eight feet from history.

"That putt, I could have hit it with my shoe and it would have gone in," Janzen said.

Stewart's last chance was to hole out the bunker shot. It was impossible. He exploded out to 15 feet and made the putt. Janzen could two-putt and win. Instead, he stepped up and dropped the eight-footer right in the middle of the hole.

Stewart immediately walked over, put his arm around Janzen's shoulder and shook his hand. Stewart is getting very good at this. It was his fourth runner-up finish of the year. Seven times in 1993 he began the final round within four shots of the lead, and hadn't won yet.

"I'll just keep knocking on the door," he said. "One of these days, that door is going to be open and I'm going to bust right through it."

Moments later, after the world's longest hug with his wife, Beverly, in the scorer's trailer, Janzen was standing on the green. He held the Open trophy aloft. He tried to speak. "I hope I can say ... I was never ... never sure I had it in me to do this ... I just feel like the luckiest man alive."

His face was reflected in the cup. Tears rolled down his cheeks.

"I didn't think I could even dream this big," he said. "This is more than a dream."

93rd U.S. Open
The Champion

Nobody who knew him was surprised. Not his teacher. Not his wife. Not his best buddy on tour. Not his mother. Not his caddie.

Every person who was close to Lee Janzen, the 28-year-old pro who birdied three of the last five holes and cooly withstood the challenge of Payne Stewart to win the 1993 U.S. Open, knew he had it in him.

Start with Rick Smith, the teaching pro who 15 years ago gave Janzen a few tips during a casual round of golf in Orlando. At the time, Janzen, 13, had been playing for about a year and was still having trouble breaking 95. Smith was visiting his brother at nearby Florida Southern and took pity on the kid.

He adjusted Janzen's set-up and alignment. Two weeks later, Janzen shot 75. The player/coach relationship that has continued to this day was formed, and has endured, because the two communicate so easily.

"There was never any doubt that Lee was a good athlete," said Smith, who is now director of golf at Treetops Resort in Gaylord, Michigan, and who also coaches PGA Tour players Rocco Mediate and Billy Andrade — not to mention Jack Nicklaus. "Plus, he had a tremendous ability to grasp things. He's very tough mentally. I think he showed that to everyone this week. That's something that stands out. You have to have that to win the Open.

"There was never a doubt in my mind that he would succeed."

How was anyone to know it would be such a high success and in such a short period of time? There was nothing about

A tearful Lee Janzen clutched his prize — the U.S. Open trophy.

Janzen's U.S. Open record to suggest it. He had missed the cut in three previous tries. His lowest round in the Open before this year was 74. His stroke average was 76.5.

Now, ask yourself this: A guy with a U.S. Open stroke average somewhere around the mean nighttime temperature of Bermuda is going to come in and shoot four rounds in the 60s in the U.S. Open? Lee Janzen doing what only Lee Trevino had done before, at the 1968 Open at Oak Hill? Is that some kind of joke, or what?

Here's a little inside joke. Janzen and his caddie have a routine they go through when they get to a course. They arrive there, look around and say, "No way we can play here, we're dead." When they do that, Janzen usually plays well. What was the first thing they said when they saw Baltusrol?

"No way," Janzen said, grinning.

Way. His play at Baltusrol was a continuation of the strides he had made all year, a year in which he won his second event (the Phoenix Open) and had six top-10 finishes, including a third at Westchester the week before the Open. But the road to the Open win began long before that. It started back when Janzen was growing up, playing Little League baseball, playing tag around the house. He had the drive to succeed even then.

"There has never been a doubt in my mind that if Lee Janzen decided to do something that he was going to accomplish it," said Nancy Janzen, Lee's mother. "He's always been willing to pay any price to get there."

Charley Matlock was Janzen's coach at Florida Southern. He saw the young man move from immaturity to maturity in a very short time. To him, Janzen's commitment

to seriously apply himself was the first clue.

"Like a lot of college kids, Lee didn't mind going to a party," Matlock said, "but he made up his mind that the only way he was going to improve as a player was if he really committed himself. He did that. That was the way he chose to go. The results are right there to see."

Janzen's dedication to commit to a change were never more apparent — nor were the fruits ever more abundant — than when he went to Smith during the week of the 1990 Open at Medinah. He had realized during the Western Open that he didn't have enough game to compete. He was driving the ball wildly, and he knew that he could never win a championship of consequence from the rough. He worked with Smith on rerouting his swing to a more down-the-line path and tightening his leg action to eliminate superfluous movement of his upper body.

It felt odd, but it worked. The next week, he finished seventh. That was his first official top 10 on the PGA Tour. His next event he finished 12th. People on the PGA Tour, who already had taken note of his extraordinary short game and exquisite putting stroke, were starting to note that his long game was looking good, too. He was still two seasons away from winning, but he was impossible to ignore.

Cut to the practice tee at Riviera Country Club, just before the 1993 Los Angeles Open. Ben Crenshaw was sitting on a bench behind the range, sizing up the young talent beating balls in front of him. He was particularly impressed with a young man

Lee Janzen "looked like a winner," said his friend, Rocco Mediate.

Lee Janzen embraced his caddie on the 18th green.

with a shock of curls spilling from beneath a baseball cap that advertises non-alcoholic beer.

"That Lee Janzen," Crenshaw said. "Now that's some very fine action right there. That's about as good as you'll see."

There are players with fine action and plenty of ability and mental toughness who turn to jelly when the United States Golf Association flag goes up the flagpole. But there was something about Janzen's bearing, even before he had success on the PGA Tour, that told golf insiders he was destined for something big.

His friend and former teammate Rocco Mediate saw it. The two played a lot of golf together in college, spent a lot of time together in Smith's company on the Tour, and something told Mediate his friend was on the verge.

"I'm not sure exactly what it was," Mediate said. "But I just could see, the way he was rolling the ball, the way he was walking, he just looked like a winner."

Then he played like one. Lee Janzen became the winner of the 93rd U.S. Open by combining breaks and bravado, ability and endurance, talent and tolerance for the vagaries of the game. Where his place in history will ultimately be is unclear. Two of the past Open champions at Baltusrol — Tony Manero and Ed Furgol — never won another major.

Now, if that were to happen to Janzen, that would be the real surprise.

"Lee is one of those special people who just keeps on improving, even when he's playing well," Smith said. "He's never been satisfied, and I don't think he'll be satisfied now, and that is what it takes to go on and keep winning major championships."

93rd U.S. Open Results

June 17-20, 1993, Baltusrol Golf Club, Springfield, New Jersey

Contestant	Rounds				Total	Prize
Lee Janzen	67	67	69	69	272	$290,000.00
Payne Stewart	70	66	68	70	274	145,000.00
Craig Parry	66	74	69	68	277	78,556.50
Paul Azinger	71	68	69	69	277	78,556.50
Scott Hoch	66	72	72	68	278	48,730.00
Tom Watson	70	66	73	69	278	48,730.00
Ernie Els	71	73	68	67	279	35,481.25
Raymond Floyd	68	73	70	68	279	35,481.25
Nolan Henke	72	71	67	69	279	35,481.25
Fred Funk	70	72	67	70	279	35,481.25
Loren Roberts	70	70	71	69	280	26,249.20
Jeff Sluman	71	71	69	69	280	26,249.20
John Adams	70	70	69	71	280	26,249.20
David Edwards	70	72	66	72	280	26,249.20
Nick Price	71	66	70	73	280	26,249.20
Barry Lane	74	68	70	69	281	21,576.67
Fred Couples	68	71	71	71	281	21,576.67
Mike Standly	70	69	70	72	281	21,576.67
Blaine McCallister	68	73	73	68	282	18,071.67
Dan Forsman	73	71	70	68	282	18,071.67
Corey Pavin	68	69	75	70	282	18,071.67
Tom Lehman	71	70	71	70	282	18,071.67
Steve Pate	70	71	71	70	282	18,071.67
Ian Baker-Finch	70	70	70	72	282	18,071.67
Curtis Strange	73	68	75	67	283	14,531.50
Naomichi Ozaki	70	70	74	69	283	14,531.50
Rocco Mediate	68	72	73	70	283	14,531.50
Chip Beck	72	68	72	71	283	14,531.50
Kenny Perry	74	70	68	71	283	14,531.50
Mark Calcavecchia	70	70	71	72	283	14,531.50
John Cook	75	66	70	72	283	14,531.50
Wayne Levi	71	69	69	74	283	14,531.50
Steve Lowery	72	71	75	66	284	11,051.85
Colin Montgomerie	71	72	73	68	284	11,051.85
Bob Gilder	70	69	75	70	284	11,051.85
Masashi Ozaki	71	71	72	70	284	11,051.85
Greg Twiggs	72	72	70	70	284	11,051.85
Billy Andrade	72	67	74	71	284	11,051.85
Lee Rinker	70	72	71	71	284	11,051.85
John Daly	72	68	72	72	284	11,051.85
Craig Stadler	67	74	71	72	284	11,051.85
Robert Allenby	74	69	69	72	284	11,051.85
Davis Love III	70	74	68	72	284	11,051.85
Steve Elkington	71	70	69	74	284	11,051.85
Mike Donald	71	72	67	74	284	11,051.85
Scott Simpson	70	73	72	70	285	8,179.17
Mark Brooks	72	68	74	71	285	8,179.17
Mark McCumber	70	71	73	71	285	8,179.17
Brian Claar	71	70	72	72	285	8,179.17
Rick Fehr	71	72	70	72	285	8,179.17

Contestant	Rounds				Total	Prize
Larry Nelson	70	71	71	73	285	8,179.17
Kirk Triplett	70	72	75	69	286	6,525.60
Ian Woosnam	70	74	72	70	286	6,525.60
Fulton Allem	71	70	74	71	286	6,525.60
Vance Heafner	70	72	73	71	286	6,525.60
Edward Kirby	72	71	72	71	286	6,525.60
Michael Christie	70	74	71	71	286	6,525.60
Keith Clearwater	71	72	71	72	286	6,525.60
Sandy Lyle	70	74	70	72	286	6,525.60
Bob Estes	71	73	69	73	286	6,525.60
Jeff Maggert	69	70	73	74	286	6,525.60
Mike Hulbert	71	73	72	71	287	5,940.50
Hale Irwin	73	71	71	72	287	5,940.50
Mike Smith	68	72	74	73	287	5,940.50
Arden Knoll	71	70	73	73	287	5,940.50
Joel Edwards	71	73	70	73	287	5,940.50
Jay Don Blake	72	70	71	74	287	5,940.50
Fuzzy Zoeller	73	67	78	70	288	5,657.00
Steve Gotsche	70	73	71	74	288	5,657.00
*Justin Leonard	69	71	73	75	288	Medal
Brad Faxon	72	71	70	75	288	5,657.00
Jack Nicklaus	70	72	76	71	289	5,405.00
Nick Faldo	70	74	73	72	289	5,405.00
Grant Waite	69	73	74	73	289	5,405.00
Pete Jordan	71	70	73	75	289	5,405.00
Duffy Waldorf	71	72	71	75	289	5,405.00
Mark Wiebe	71	72	77	70	290	5,121.50
Tony Johnstone	71	72	74	73	290	5,121.50
Jay Haas	71	69	75	75	290	5,121.50
Barney Thompson	71	73	71	75	290	5,121.50
Wayne Grady	69	75	70	77	291	4,932.50
Ted Schulz	71	73	69	78	291	4,932.50
Steve Stricker	72	72	76	72	292	4,838.00
Stephen Flesch	71	70	78	75	294	4,775.00
Doug Weaver	70	73	77	75	295	4,680.50
John Flannery	73	69	75	78	295	4,680.50
Robert Wrenn	68	73	80	76	297	4,586.00
Robert Gamez	72	70	78	78	298	4,523.00

Jim Gallagher, Jr.	74-71—145	Howard Twitty	71-76—147	Carlos Espinosa	76-74—150
Gil Morgan	73-72—145	Peter Jacobsen	76-71—147	Edward Whitman	73-77—150
Bernhard Langer	74-71—145	Greg Norman	73-74—147	*David Berganio	74-76—150
Masahiro Kuramoto	72-73—145	Andy North	77-70—147	Tad Rhyan	73-77—150
Joey Sindelar	66-79—145	Bruce Vaughan	75-72—147	Mark Pfeil	77-73—150
Vijay Singh	73-72—145	Larry Mize	73-74—147	Todd Erwin	76-75—151
Tom Kite	75-70—145	Mike Springer	77-71—148	Darryl Court	76-75—151
Tom Sipula	72-73—145	Tom Woodard	72-76—148	David Peoples	77-74—151
Mark Mielke	72-73—145	Jerry Smith	72-76—148	Bob Tway	72-79—151
Michael Clark	72-73—145	David Frost	72-76—148	Eric Hoos	75-76—151
Michael Weeks	69-76—145	D.A. Weibring	76-72—148	Rick Cramer	73-79—152
Brad Fabel	73-72—145	Jose Maria Olazabal	74-74—148	Oswald Drawdy	74-78—152
Bill Glasson	69-76—145	Seve Ballesteros	76-72—148	Gene Fieger	81-71—152
Kevin Wentworth	71-74—145	Russ Cochran	71-77—148	Billy Tuten	73-79—152
Dave Barr	71-74—145	Bill Britton	76-72—148	Kevin Altenhoff	81-72—153
Barry Cheesman	73-72—145	Mark Balen	77-71—148	Javier Sanchez	78-77—155
Mike Colandro	78-67—145	Jeff McMillan	79-69—148	*Ted Oh	76-79—155
Kelly Gibson	71-75—146	Anders Forsbrand	77-72—149	David Brown	78-79—157
Kevin Burton	74-72—146	David Gilford	73-76—149	Mark O'Meara	80-78—158
Sean Murphy	72-74—146	John Mahaffey	78-71—149	Mark Singer	77-82—159
Roger Maltbie	75-71—146	Kevin Giancola	76-74—150	Jim Hallet	82-79—161
Dick Mast	72-74—146	John Huston	72-78—150	Kevin Roman	81-84—165
Willie Wood	73-73—146	Jim Thorpe	77-73—150		

Professionals not returning 72-hole scores received $1,000 each.   *Denotes amateur.

93rd U.S. Open Statistics

Hole	1	2	3	4	5	6	7	8	9	10	11	12	13	14	15	16	17	18	Total	
Par	4	4	4	3	4	4	4	4	3	4	4	3	4	4	4	3	5	5	70	
Lee Janzen																				
Round 1	3	4	5	3	3	4	4	4	2	4	3	3	4	4	5	3	5	4	67	
Round 2	5	4	4	3	4	3	4	4	3	4	3	2	3	4	4	3	5	5	67	
Round 3	3	3	5	3	5	4	4	3	3	4	4	3	4	4	5	3	5	4	69	
Round 4	4	5	3	3	4	4	5	4	3	4	4	4	4	3	4	2	5	4	69	272
Payne Stewart																				
Round 1	4	4	4	3	4	4	5	4	3	4	3	3	4	4	4	2	5	6	70	
Round 2	4	4	4	3	4	3	4	4	2	4	4	2	4	4	3	3	6	4	66	
Round 3	4	4	4	3	4	4	4	4	3	4	4	3	3	4	4	3	5	4	68	
Round 4	5	4	4	3	4	4	5	4	2	4	4	3	4	4	4	3	5	4	70	274
Paul Azinger																				
Round 1	4	4	4	3	4	4	4	5	4	3	3	3	5	4	3	4	4	6	71	
Round 2	5	4	4	3	4	4	4	3	2	5	5	3	4	3	3	2	6	4	68	
Round 3	4	4	3	3	4	4	4	4	4	4	4	3	4	4	5	3	4	4	69	
Round 4	5	3	3	3	4	5	5	4	3	4	3	3	4	4	4	3	5	4	69	277
Craig Parry																				
Round 1	4	3	3	3	4	5	3	4	3	3	4	4	4	3	4	3	4	5	66	
Round 2	5	4	4	4	5	4	4	4	3	4	4	3	5	4	4	3	5	5	74	
Round 3	3	4	4	3	3	5	4	4	3	4	3	4	4	4	4	4	4	5	69	
Round 4	4	4	4	4	3	4	4	4	3	4	6	3	3	3	4	3	4	4	68	277

Hole	Yards	Par	Eagles	Birdies	Pars	Bogeys	Higher	Average
1	470	4	0	45	288	137	18	4.262
2	381	4	0	45	348	88	7	4.116
3	466	4	0	42	305	128	13	4.235
4	194	3	0	65	337	74	12	3.069
5	413	4	0	39	316	123	10	4.213
6	470	4	0	34	304	141	9	4.260
7	470	4	0	37	283	150	18	4.309
8	374	4	0	64	341	79	4	4.047
9	205	3	0	47	335	94	12	3.145
OUT	3443	34	0	418	2857	1014	103	35.656
10	454	4	0	50	332	101	5	4.127
11	428	4	0	39	295	142	12	4.262
12	193	3	2	49	350	81	6	3.081
13	401	4	0	71	322	84	11	4.071
14	415	4	0	73	350	61	4	3.991
15	430	4	0	45	320	115	8	4.178
16	216	3	0	53	350	81	4	3.073
17	630	5	0	88	332	59	9	4.977
18	542	5	9	186	247	42	4	4.684
IN	3709	36	11	654	2898	766	63	36.444
TOTAL	7152	70	11	1072	5755	1780	166	72.100

93rd U.S. Open
Past Results

Date	Winner, Runner-Up	Score	Site	Entry
1895 (Oct.)	**Horace Rawlins** Willie Dunn	173 175	**Newport G.C.,** Newport R.I.	11
1896 (July)	**James Foulis** Horace Rawlins	†152 155	**Shinnecock Hills G.C.,** Southampton, N.Y.	35
1897 (Sept.)	**Joe Lloyd** Willie Anderson	162 163	**Chicago G.C.,** Wheaton, Ill.	35
1898 (June)	**Fred Herd** Alex Smith	328 335	**Myopia Hunt Club,** S. Hamilton, Mass.	49
1899 (Sept.)	**Willie Smith** George Low/Val Fitzjohn/W.H. Way	315 326	**Baltimore C.C.,** (Roland Park Course) Baltimore, Md.	81
1900 (Oct.)	**Harry Vardon** J.H. Taylor	313 315	**Chicago G.C.,** Wheaton, Ill.	60
1901 (June)	**Willie Anderson** Alex Smith	331-85 331-86	**Myopia Hunt Club,** S. Hamilton, Mass.	60
1902 (Oct.)	**Lawrence Auchterlonie** Stewart Gardner/*Walter J. Travis	307 313	**Garden City G.C.,** Garden City, N.Y.	90
1903 (June)	**Willie Anderson** David Brown	307-82 307-84	**Baltusrol G.C.,** (original course) Springfield, N.J.	89
1904 (July)	**Willie Anderson** Gilbert Nicholls	303 308	**Glen View Club,** Golf, Ill.	71
1905 (Sept.)	**Willie Anderson** Alex Smith	314 316	**Myopia Hunt Club,** S. Hamilton, Mass.	83
1906 (June)	**Alex Smith** William Smith	295 302	**Onwentsia Club,** Lake Forest, Ill.	68
1907 (June)	**Alex Ross** Gilbert Nicholls	302 304	**Philadelphia Cricket C.,** (St. Martins Course) Philadelphia, Pa.	82
1908 (Aug.)	**Fred McLeod** Willie Smith	322-77 322-83	**Myopia Hunt Club,** S. Hamilton, Mass.	88
1909 (June)	**George Sargent** Tom McNamara	290 294	**Englewood G.C.,** Englewood, N.Y.	84
1910 (June)	**Alex Smith** John J. McDermott Macdonald Smith	298-71 298-75 298-77	**Philadelphia Cricket C.,** (St. Martins Course) Philadelphia, Pa.	75
1911 (June)	**John J. McDermott** Michael J. Brady George O. Simpson	307-80 307-82 307-85	**Chicago G.C.,** Wheaton, Ill.	79
1912 (Aug.)	**John J. McDermott** Tom McNamara	294 296	**C.C. of Buffalo** Buffalo, N.Y.	131
1913 (Sept.)	***Francis Ouimet** Harry Vardon Edward Ray	304-72 304-77 304-78	**The Country Club** Brookline, Mass.	165
1914 (Aug.)	**Walter Hagen** *Charles Evans, Jr.	290 291	**Midlothian C.C.,** Blue Island, Ill.	129
1915 (June)	***Jerone D. Travers** Tom McNamara	297 298	**Baltusrol G.C.,** (original course,) Springfield, N.J.	141
1916 (June)	***Charles Evans, Jr.** Jock Hutchinson	286 288	**Minikahda Club,** Minneapolis, Minn.	94
1917-18 — No Championships: World War I				
1919 (June)	**Walter Hagen** Michael J. Brady	301-77 301-78	**Brae Burn C.C.,** West Newton, Mass.	142
1920 (Aug.)	**Edward Ray** Harry Vardon/Jack Burke, Sr./ Leo Diegel/Jock Hutchison	295 296	**Inverness Club,** Toledo, Ohio	265
1921 (July)	**James M. Barnes** Walter Hagen/Fred McLeod	289 298	**Columbia C.C.,** Chevy Chase, Md.	262
1922 (July)	**Gene Sarazen** *Robert T. Jones, Jr./John L. Black	288 289	**Skokie C.C.,** Glencoe, Ill.	323
1923 (July)	***Robert T. Jones, Jr.** Bobby Cruickshank	296-76 296-78	**Inwood C.C.,** Inwood, N.Y.	360

Past Results

Date	Winner, Runner-Up	Score	Site	Entry
1924 (June)	**Cyril Walker**	297	**Oakland Hills C.C.,**	319
	*Robert T. Jones, Jr.	300	(South Course) Birmingham, Mich.	
1925 (June)	**William Macfarlane**	291-75-72	**Worcester C.C.,**	445
	*Robert T. Jones, Jr.	291-75-73	Worcester, Mass.	
1926 (June)	***Robert T. Jones, Jr.**	293	**Scioto C.C.,**	694
	Joe Turnesa	294	Columbus, Ohio	
1927 (June)	**Tommy Armour**	301-76	**Oakmont C.C.,**	898
	Harry Cooper	301-79	Oakmont, Pa.	
1928 (June)	**Johnny Farrell**	294-143	**Olympia Fields C.C.,**	1,064
	*Robert T. Jones, Jr.	294-144	(No. 4 Course) Mateson, Ill.	
1929 (June)	***Robert T. Jones, Jr.**	294-141	**Winged Foot G.C.,**	1,000
	Al Espinosa	294-164	(West Course) Mamaroneck, N.Y.	
1930 (July)	***Robert T. Jones, Jr.**	287	**Interlachen C.C.,**	1,177
	Macdonald Smith	289	Minneapolis, Minn.	
1931 (July)	**Billy Burke**	292-149-148	**Inverness Club,**	1,141
	George Von Elm	292-149-149	Toledo, Ohio	
1932 (June)	**Gene Sarazen**	286	**Fresh Meadow C.C.,**	1,011
	Bobby Cruickshank/T. Philip Perkins	289	Flushing, N.Y.	
1933 (June)	***John Goodman**	287	**North Shore C.C.,**	915
	Ralph Guldahl	288	Glenview, Ill.	
1934 (June)	**Olin Dutra**	293	**Merion Cricket C.,**	1,063
	Gene Sarazen	294	(East Course) Ardmore, Pa.	
1935 (June)	**Sam Parks, Jr.**	299	**Oakmont C.C.,**	1,125
	Jimmy Thomson	301	Oakmont, Pa.	
1936 (June)	**Tony Manero**	282	**Baltusrol G.C.,**	1,277
	Harry Cooper	284	(Upper Course) Springfield, N.Y.	
1937 (June)	**Ralph Guldahl**	281	**Oakland Hills C.C.,**	1,402
	Sam Snead	283	(South Course) Birmingham, Mich.	
1938 (June)	**Ralph Guldahl**	284	**Cherry Hills C.C.,**	1,223
	Dick Metz	290	Englewood, Colo.	
1939 (June)	**Byron Nelson**	284-68-70	**Philadelphia C.C.,**	1,193
	Craig Wood	284-68-73	(Spring Mill Course)	
	Denny Shute	284-76	West Conshohocken, Pa.	
1940 (June)	**Lawson Little**	287-70	**Canterbury C.C.,**	1,161
	Gene Sarazen	287-73	Cleveland, Ohio	
1941 (June)	**Craig Wood**	284	**Colonial Club,**	1,048
	Denny Shute	287	Fort Worth, Tex.	
1942-45 — No Championships: World War II				
1946 (June)	**Lloyd Mangrum**	284-72-72	**Canterbury C.C.,**	1,175
	Byron Nelson/Victor Ghezzi	284-72-73	Cleveland, Ohio	
1947 (June)	**Lew Worsham**	282-69	**St. Louis G.C.,**	1,356
	Sam Snead	282-70	Clayton, Mo.	
1948 (June)	**Ben Hogan**	276	**Riviera C.C.,**	1,411
	Jimmy Demaret	278	Los Angeles, Calif.	
1949 (June)	**Cary Middlecoff**	286	**Medinah C.C.,**	1,348
	Sam Snead/Clayton Heafner	287	(No. 3 Course) Medinah, Ill.	
1950 (June)	**Ben Hogan**	287-69	**Merion G.C.,**	1,379
	Lloyd Mangrum	287-73	(East Course) Ardmore, Pa.	
	George Fazio	287-75		
1951 (June)	**Ben Hogan**	287	**Oakland Hills C.C.,**	1,511
	Clayton Heafner	289	(South Course) Birmingham, Mich.	
1952 (June)	**Julius Boros**	281	**Northwood Club,**	1,688
	Ed (Porky) Oliver	285	Dallas, Tex.	
1953 (June)	**Ben Hogan**	283	**Oakmont C.C.,**	1,669
	Sam Snead	289	Oakmont, Pa.	
1954 (June)	**Ed Furgol**	284	**Baltusrol G.C.,**	1,928
	Gene Littler	285	(Lower Course) Springfield, N. J.	
1955 (June)	**Jack Fleck**	287-69	**Olympic Club,**	1,522
	Ben Hogan	287-72	(Lake Course) San Francisco, Calif.	
1956 (June)	**Cary Middlecoff**	281	**Oak Hill C.C.,**	1,921
	Julius Boros/Ben Hogan	282	(East Course) Rochester, N.Y.	
1957 (June)	**Dick Mayer**	282-72	**Inverness Club,**	1,907
	Cary Middlecoff	282-79	Toledo, Ohio	
1958 (June)	**Tommy Bolt**	283	**Southern Hills C.C.,**	2,132
	Gary Player	287	Tulsa, Okla.	
1959 (June)	**Bill Casper, Jr.**	282	**Winged Foot G.C.,**	2,385
	Bob Rosburg	283	(West Course) Mamaroneck, N.Y.	
1960 (June)	**Arnold Palmer**	280	**Cherry Hills C.C.,**	2,453
	*Jack Nicklaus	282	Englewood, Colo.	

Date	Winners, Runner-Up	Score	Site	Entry
1961 (June)	**Gene Littler**	281	**Oakland Hills C.C.,**	2,449
	Doug Sanders/Bob Goalby	282	(South Course) Birmingham, Mich.	
1962 (June)	**Jack Nicklaus**	283-71	**Oakmont C.C.,**	2,475
	Arnold Palmer	283-74	Oakmont, Pa.	
1963 (June)	**Julius Boros**	293-70	**The Country Club**	2,392
	Jacky Cupit	293-73	Brookline, Mass.	
	Arnold Palmer	293-76		
1964 (June)	**Ken Venturi**	278	**Congressional C.C.,**	2,341
	Tommy Jacobs	282	Washington, D.C.	
1965 (June)	**Gary Player**	282-71	**Bellerive C.C.,**	2,271
	Kel Nagel	282-74	St. Louis, Mo.	
1966 (June)	**Bill Casper, Jr.**	278-69	**Olympic Club,**	2,475
	Arnold Palmer	278-73	(Lake Course) San Francisco, Calif.	
1967 (June)	**Jack Nicklaus**	275	**Baltusrol G.C.,**	2,651
	Arnold Palmer	279	(Lower Course) Springfield, N.J.	
1968 (June)	**Lee Trevino**	275	**Oak Hill C.C.,**	3,007
	Jack Nicklaus	279	(East Course) Rochester, N.Y.	
1969 (June)	**Orville Moody**	281	**Champions G.C.,**	3,397
	Deane Beman/Al Geiberger/Bob Rosburg	282	(Cypress Creek Course) Houston, Tex.	
1970 (June)	**Tony Jacklin**	281	**Hazeltine National G.C.,**	3,605
	Dave Hill	288	Chaska, Minn.	
1971 (June)	**Lee Trevino**	280-68	**Merion G.C.,**	4,279
	Jack Nicklaus	280-71	(East Course) Ardmore, Pa.	
1972 (June)	**Jack Nicklaus**	290	**Pebble Beach G.L.,**	4,196
	Bruce Crampton	293	Pebble Beach, Calif.	
1973 (June)	**John Miller**	279	**Oakmont C.C.,**	3,580
	John Schlee	280	Oakmont, Pa.	
1974 (June)	**Hale Irwin**	287	**Winged Foot G.C.,**	3,914
	Forrest Fezler	289	(West Course) Mamaroneck, N.Y.	
1975 (June)	**Lou Graham**	287-71	**Medinah C.C.,**	4,214
	John Mahaffey	287-73	(No. 3 Course) Medinah, Ill.	
1976 (June)	**Jerry Pate**	277	**Atlanta Athletic C.,**	4,436
	Tom Weiskopf/Al Geiberger	279	Duluth, Ga.	
1977 (June)	**Hubert Green**	278	**Southern Hills C.C.,**	4,608
	Lou Graham	279	Tulsa, Okla.	
1978 (June)	**Andy North**	285	**Cherry Hills C.C.,**	4,897
	J.C. Snead/Dave Stockton	286	Englewood, Colo.	
1979 (June)	**Hale Irwin**	284	**Inverness Club,**	4,853
	Gary Player/Jerry Pate	286	Toledo, Ohio	
1980 (June)	**Jack Nicklaus**	†272	**Baltusrol G.C.,**	4,812
	Isao Aoki	274	(Lower Course) Springfield, N. J.	
1981 (June)	**David Graham**	273	**Merion G.C.,**	4,946
	Bill Rogers/George Burns	276	(East Course) Ardmore, Pa.	
1982 (June)	**Tom Watson**	282	**Pebble Beach G.L.,**	5,255
	Jack Nicklaus	284	Pebble Beach, Calif.	
1983 (June)	**Larry Nelson**	280	**Oakmont C.C.,**	5,039
	Tom Watson	281	Oakmont, Pa.	
1984 (June)	**Fuzzy Zoeller**	276-67	**Winged Foot G.C.,**	5,195
	Greg Norman	276-75	(West Course) Mamaroneck, N.Y.	
1985 (June)	**Andy North**	279	**Oakland Hills C.C.,**	5,274
	Chen Tze-Chung/Denis Watson/Dave Barr	280	(South Course) Birmingham, Mich.	
1986 (June)	**Raymond Floyd**	279	**Shinnecock Hills G.C.,**	5,410
	Lanny Wadkins/Chip Beck	281	Southampton, N.Y.	
1987 (June)	**Scott Simpson**	277	**Olympic Club,**	5,696
	Tom Watson	278	(Lake Course) San Francisco, Calif.	
1988 (June)	**Curtis Strange**	278-71	**The Country Club,**	5,775
	Nick Faldo	278-75	Brookline, Mass.	
1989 (June)	**Curtis Strange**	278	**Oak Hill C.C.,**	5,786
	Chip Beck/Mark McCumber/Ian Woosnam	279	(East Course) Rochester, N.Y.	
1990 (June)	**Hale Irwin**	280-74/3	**Medinah C.C.,**	6,198
	Mike Donald	280-74/4	(No. 3 Course) Medinah, Ill.	
1991 (June)	**Payne Stewart**	282-75	**Hazeltine National G.C.,**	6,063
	Scott Simpson	282-77	Chaska, Minn.	
1992 (June)	**Tom Kite**	285	**Pebble Beach G.L.,**	§6,244
	Jeff Sluman	287	Pebble Beach, Calif.	
1993 (June)	**Lee Janzen**	†272	**Baltusrol G.C.,**	5,905
	Payne Stewart	274	(Lower Course) Springfield, N. J.	

†Record Score *Denotes Amateur § Record Entry

93rd U.S. Open Championship Records

Oldest champion (years/months/days)
  45/0/15 — Hale Irwin (1990)
Youngest champion
  19/10/14 — John J. McDermott (1911)
Most victories
  4 — Willie Anderson (1901, 03, 04, 05)
  4 — Robert T. Jones, Jr. (1923, 26, 29, 30)
  4 — Ben Hogan (1948, 50, 51, 53)
  4 — Jack Nicklaus (1962, 67, 72, 80)
  3 — Hale Irwin (1974, 79, 90)
  2 — by 11 players: Alex Smith (1906, 10), John J. McDermott (1911, 12), Walter Hagen (1914, 19), Gene Sarazen (1922, 32), Ralph Guldahl (1937, 38), Cary Middlecoff (1949, 56), Julius Boros (1952, 63), Bill Casper (1959, 66), Lee Trevino (1968, 71), Andy North (1978, 85), and Curtis Strange (1988, 89).
Consecutive victories
  Willie Anderson (1903, 04, 05)
  John J. McDermott (1911, 12)
  Robert T. Jones, Jr. (1929, 30)
  Ralph Guldahl (1937, 38)
  Ben Hogan (1950, 51)
  Curtis Strange (1988, 89)
Most times runner-up
  4 — Sam Snead
  4 — Robert T. Jones, Jr.
  4 — Arnold Palmer
  4 — Jack Nicklaus
Longest course
  7,195 yards — Medinah C.C. (No. 3 Course), Medinah, Ill. (1990)
Shortest course
  Since World War II
  6,528 yards — Merion G.C. (East Course), Ardmore, Pa. (1971, 81)
Most often host club of Open
  7 — Baltusrol G.C., Springfield, N.J. (1903, 15, 36, 54, 67, 80, 93)
  6 — Oakmont (Pa.) C.C. (1927, 35, 53, 62, 73, 83)
Largest entry
  6,244 (1992)
Smallest entry
  11 (1895)
Lowest score, 72 holes
  272 — Jack Nicklaus (63-71-70-68), at Baltusrol G.C. (Lower Course), Springfield, N.J. (1980)
  272 — Lee Janzen (67-67-69-69), at Baltusrol G.C. (Lower Course), Springfield, N.J. (1993)
Lowest score, first 54 holes
  203 — George Burns (69-66-68), at Merion G.C. (East Course), Ardmore, Pa. (1981)
  203 — Chen Tze-Chung (65-69-69), at Oakland Hills C.C. (South Course), Birmingham, Mich. (1985)
  203 — Lee Janzen (67-67-69), at Baltusrol G.C. (Lower Course), Springfield, N.J. (1993)
Lowest score, last 54 holes
  204 — Jack Nicklaus (67-72-65), at Baltusrol G.C. (Lower Course), Springfield, N.J. (1967)
  204 — Raymond Floyd (68-70-66), at Shinnecock Hills G.C., Southampton, N.Y. (1986)
Lowest score, first 36 holes
  134 — Jack Nicklaus (63-71), at Baltusrol G.C. (Lower Course), Springfield, N.J. (1980)
  134 — Chen Tze-Chung (65-69), at Oakland Hills C.C. (South Course), Birmingham, Mich. (1985)
  134 — Lee Janzen (67-67), at Baltusrol G.C. (Lower Course), Springfield, N.J. (1993)
Lowest score, last 36 holes
  132 — Larry Nelson (65-67), at Oakmont C.C., Oakmont, Pa. (1983)
Lowest score, 9 holes
  30 — on 15 occasions, most recently by Andy Dillard (first nine, first round) at Pebble Beach (Calif.) Golf Links (1992)
Lowest score, 18 holes
  63 — Johnny Miller, fourth round at Oakmont (Pa.) C.C. (1973)
  63 — Jack Nicklaus, first round at Baltusrol G.C. (Lower Course), Springfield, N.J. (1980)
  63 — Tom Weiskopf, first round at Baltusrol G.C. (Lower Course), Springfield, N.J. (1980)
Largest winning margin
  11 — Willie Smith (315), at Baltimore (Md.) C.C. (Roland Park Course) (1899)
Highest winning score
  Since World War II
  293 — Julius Boros, at The Country Club, Brookline, Mass. (1963) (won in playoff)
Best start by champion
  63 — Jack Nicklaus, at Baltusrol G.C. (Lower Course), Springfield, N.J. (1980)
Best finish by champion
  63 — Johnny Miller, at Oakmont (Pa.) C.C. (1973)
Worst start by champion
  Since World War II
  76 — Ben Hogan, at Oakland Hills C.C. (South Course), Birmingham, Mich. (1951)
  76 — Jack Fleck, at The Olympic Club (Lake Course), San Francisco, Calif. (1955)

Worst finish by champion
Since World War II
  75 — Cary Middlecoff, at Medinah C.C. (No. 3 Course), Medinah, Ill. (1949)
  75 — Hale Irwin, at Inverness Club, Toledo, Ohio (1979)

Lowest score to lead field, 18 holes
  63 — Jack Nicklaus and Tom Weiskopf, at Baltusrol G.C. (Lower Course), Springfield, N.J. (1980)

Lowest score to lead field, 36 holes
  134 — Jack Nicklaus (63-71), at Baltusrol G.C. (Lower Course), Springfield, N.J. (1980)
  134 — Chen Tze-Chung (65-69), at Oakland Hills C.C. (South Course), Birmingham, Mich. (1985)
  134 — Lee Janzen (67-67), at Baltusrol G.C. (Lower Course), Springfield, N.J. (1993)

Lowest score to lead field, 54 holes
  203 — George Burns (69-66-68), at Merion G.C. (East Course), Ardmore, Pa. (1981)
  203 — Chen Tze-Chung (65-69-69), at Oakland Hills C.C. (South Course), Birmingham, Mich. (1985)
  203 — Lee Janzen (67-67-69), at Baltusrol G.C. (Lower Course), Springfield, N.J. (1993)

Highest score to lead field, 18 holes
Since World War II
  71 — Sam Snead, at Oakland Hills C.C. (South Course), Birmingham, Mich. (1951)
  71 — Tommy Bolt, Julius Boros, and Dick Metz, at Southern Hills C.C., Tulsa, Okla. (1958)
  71 — Tony Jacklin, at Hazeltine National G.C., Chaska, Minn. (1970)
  71 — Orville Moody, Jack Nicklaus, Chi Chi Rodriguez, Mason Rudolph, Tom Shaw, and Kermit Zarley, at Pebble Beach (Calif.) Golf Links (1972)

Highest score to lead field, 36 holes
Since World War II
  144 — Bobby Locke (73-71), at Oakland Hills C.C. (South Course), Birmingham, Mich. (1951)
  144 — Tommy Bolt (67-77) and E. Harvie Ward (74-70), at The Olympic Club (Lake Course), San Francisco, Calif. (1955)
  144 — Homero Blancas (74-70), Bruce Crampton (74-70), Jack Nicklaus (71-73), Cesar Seduno (72-72), Lanny Wadkins (76-68) and Kermit Zarley (71-73), at Pebble Beach (Calif.) Golf Links (1972)

Highest score to lead field, 54 holes
Since World War II
  218 — Bobby Locke (73-71-74), at Oakland Hills C.C. (South Course), Birmingham, Mich. (1951)
  218 — Jacky Cupit (70-72-76), at The Country Club, Brookline, Mass. (1963)

Highest 36-hole cut
  155 — at The Olympic Club (Lakeside Course), San Francisco, Calif. (1955)

Most players to tie for lead, 18 holes
  7 — at Pebble Beach (Calif.) Golf Links (1972); at Southern Hills C.C., Tulsa, Okla. (1977); and at Shinnecock Hills G.C., Southampton, N.Y. (1896)

Most players to tie for lead, 36 holes
  6 — at Pebble Beach (Calif.) Golf Links (1972)

Most players to tie for lead, 54 holes
  4 — at Oakmont (Pa.) C.C. (1973)

Most sub-par rounds, championship
  124 — at Medinah C.C. (No. 3 Course), Medinah, Ill. (1990)

Most sub-par 72-hole totals, championship
  28 — at Medinah C.C. (No. 3 Course), Medinah, Ill. (1990)

Most sub-par scores, first round
  39 — at Medinah C.C. (No. 3 Course), Medinah, Ill. (1990)

Most sub-par scores, second round
  47 — at Medinah C.C. (No. 3 Course), Medinah, Ill. (1990)

Most sub-par scores, third round
  24 — at Medinah C.C. (No. 3 Course), Medinah, Ill. (1990)

Most sub-par scores, fourth round
  18 — at Baltusrol G.C. (Lower Course), Springfield, N.J. (1993)

Most sub-par rounds by one player in one championship
  4 — Bill Casper, at The Olympic Club (Lakeside Course), San Francisco, Calif. (1966)
  4 — Lee Trevino, at Oak Hill C.C. (East Course), Rochester, N.Y. (1968)
  4 — Tony Jacklin, at Hazeltine National G.C., Chaska, Minn. (1970)
  4 — Lee Janzen, at Baltusrol G.C. (Lower Course), Springfield, N.J. (1993)

Highest score, one hole
  19 — Ray Ainsley, at the 16th (par 4) at Cherry Hills C.C., Englewood, Colo. (1938)

Most consecutive birdies
  6 — George Burns (holes 2–7), at Pebble Beach (Calif.) Golf Links (1972) and Andy Dillard (holes 1–6), at Pebble Beach (Calif.) Golf Links (1992)

Most consecutive 3s
  7 — Hubert Green (holes 10–16), at Southern Hills Country Club, Tulsa, Okla. (1977)
  7 — Peter Jacobsen (holes 1–7), at The Country Club, Brookline, Mass. (1988)

Most consecutive Opens
  37 — Jack Nicklaus (1957-93)

Most Opens completed 72 holes
  31 — Jack Nicklaus

Most consecutive Opens completed 72 holes
  22 — Walter Hagen (1913-36; no Championships 1917-18)
  22 — Gene Sarazen (1920-41)
  22 — Gary Player (1958-79)

Larry Dorman is the golf writer and columnist for the *Fort Lauderdale Sun-Sentinel*, a contributor to national golf magazines and author of a book on golf records.

Lawrence Levy is a photographer based in London, England, a contributor to many magazines and author of several books.

Michael C. Cohen is a photographer based in New York City and a contributor to many magazines and books.

93rd U.S. Open Championship
Baltusrol Golf Club • June 17-20, 1993

Par and Yardage

Hole	Par	Yardage	Hole	Par	Yardage
1	4	470	10	4	454
2	4	381	11	4	428
3	4	466	12	3	193
4	3	162/194	13	4	401
5	4	413	14	4	415
6	4	470	15	4	430
7	4	470	16	3	180/216
8	4	374	17	5	630
9	3	205	18	5	542
	34	3,411/3,443		36	3,673/3,709
				70	7,084/7,152

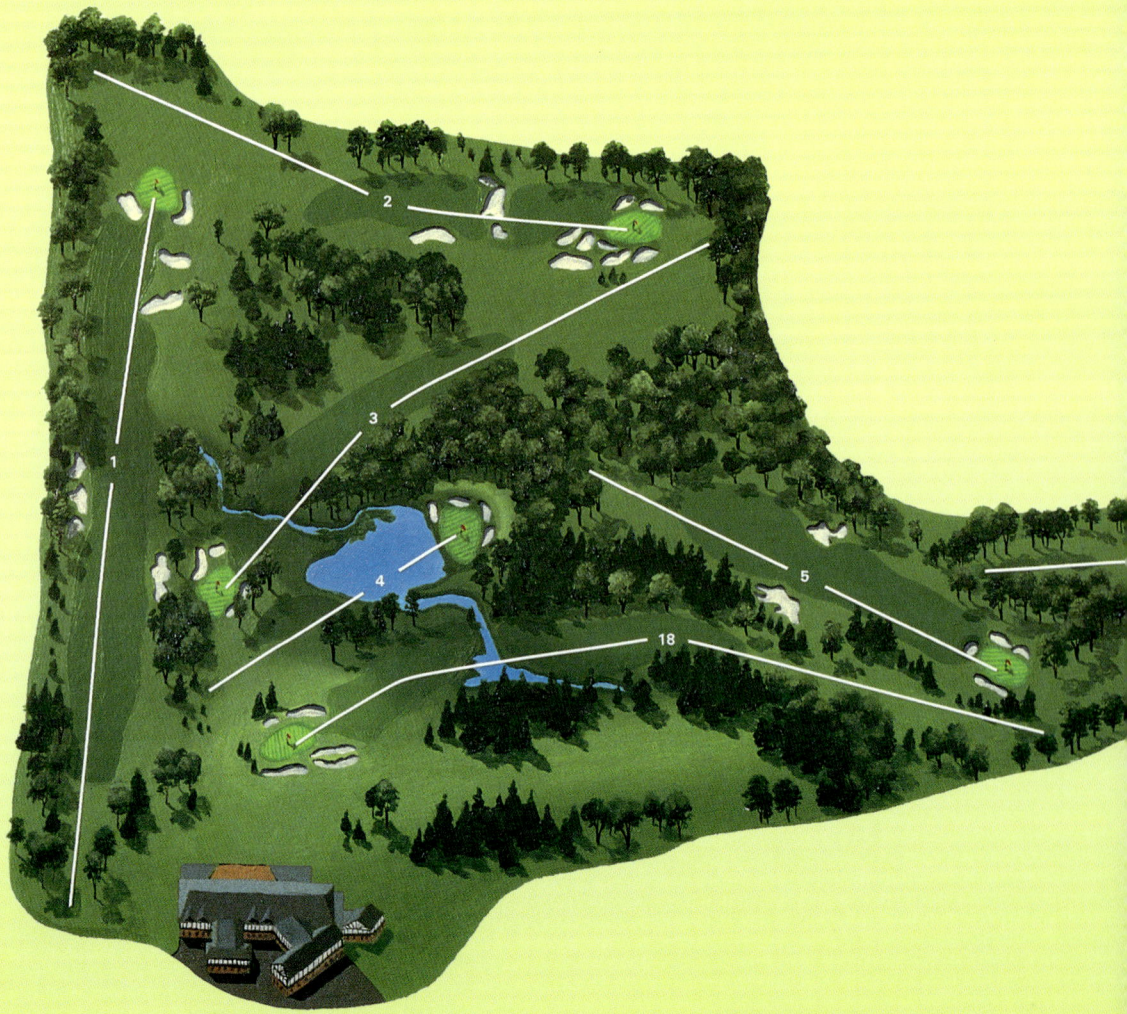